Creatures of the Woods

by Toni Eugene

A squirrel nibbles a nut it found in the woods.

BOOKS FOR YOUNG EXPLORERS
NATIONAL GEOGRAPHIC SOCIETY

In the woods, where a lot of trees grow, animals find food and places to live. They drink from a stream flowing by the trees. You may not see them, but many animals are hidden there.

2

Some make their homes on the ground.
Insects live under rocks and fallen trees.
A rabbit finds cover on the forest floor.

A male turkey and two females wander through the woods. The male is called a tom. It has a more colorful head than the females have. The females, called hens, lay eggs on the ground. They sit on them and keep them warm until the young hatch.

As a rattlesnake crawls through leaves on the ground, it may find eggs and mice. Snakes can make the forest floor a dangerous place for small animals. Many small creatures of the woods live and hide in trees. A gray squirrel watches from high on a branch. Baby squirrels a few weeks old sleep in their cozy nest in a tree.

Raccoons often use a hollow
tree as a home. Their sharp claws
and strong paws help them climb.
Raccoons eat fruits, nuts, and
small animals such as mice and frogs.

With their sharp bills, woodpeckers
peck holes in trees for their nests.
A woodpecker carries insects in its
bill. It feeds its young in the nest.

High in a tree, a pine marten looks
all around. This animal is about the size of
a small house cat. It is at home in the trees
and on the ground. Hunting for food,
it dashes after squirrels and mice.
When a woodpecker moves out of its tree
hole, a marten may move in.

A white-tailed deer stands in a shallow pond and drinks. Tiny green plants called duckweed grow on the water.

Deer must stay alert to danger. They swim well and can run very fast. In the woods, they find good hiding places.

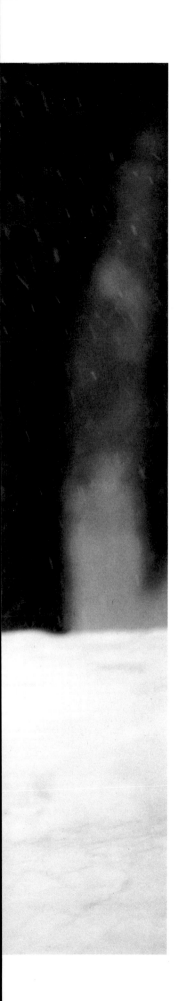

Wolves look like big dogs. They eat deer and
other animals, but they stay away from people.
Most people never see wolves in the wild.
Wolves hunt together and share their meals.
In winter, they sometimes travel for days to find food.
A wolf cleans its fur with its big pink tongue.

Big ears, sharp eyes, and a long nose help the red fox find food, even in winter. It can hear small animals moving under the snow.

Red foxes eat mice, birds, and many other things. They usually hunt alone. Foxes find safe places in the woods for their dens.

For their long winter sleep, black bears make dens in trees, in caves, or in holes they dig. There they have their young, called cubs. Snow nearly covers this den. Inside, a bear and her cubs stay safe and warm. When spring comes, the bears go outside. In the sunshine, a mother nurses her cubs.

Did you know that bears climb trees? Digging into the bark with their sharp claws, black bears can climb fast. They go up trees to eat bark, acorns, and honey. They may climb to get away from other bears or from people.

Bears can swim, too. They play in the water. They also find food there. A black bear carries a fish it caught in its big jaws.

A mountain lion naps in a tree. This big wild cat is also called a cougar. It can leap from the ground up into a tree.

Most of the time, mountain lions live alone. They find homes in many different places. They often hunt deer at night.

At times, the woods are filled with sounds. Squirrels chatter. Birds sing, and insects buzz. Animals cry out to each other. Deep in the woods, this elk is calling a mate.

An elk is a kind of deer. It eats grasses, flowers, and other plants. Colorful flowers bloom in spring. Butterflies land on the flowers and sip the sweet juice called nectar.

Some creatures come out at night and look for food.
When their mother leaves the den, baby opossums ride along.
Opossums eat grasses, fruits, nuts, worms, and even snakes.

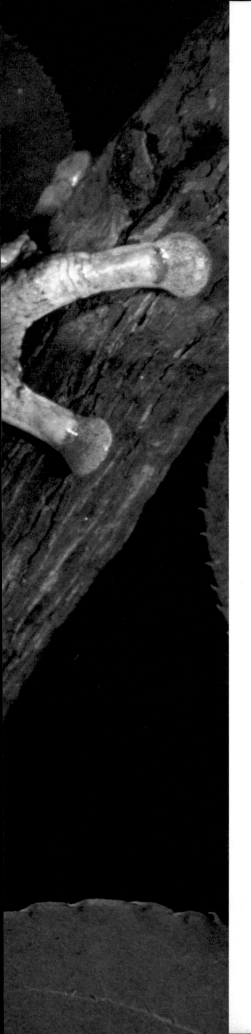

A grasshopper is a mouthful for a little tree frog. This frog is as small as your thumb. At night, it looks for insects in the trees. Other animals are hunting in the dark, too. A raccoon eats a frog it caught near a stream.

Great horned owls hunt
at night and rest during the day.
A mother owl and her two owlets
huddle in their nest. The young
are covered with soft fuzz.
They cannot fly yet. When an
owlet is afraid, it puffs up
its feathers and looks scary.

Day and night, animals are
moving about in the woods.
If you walk carefully and quietly,
you might see some of the
creatures that live there.

A gray squirrel holds on to a tree trunk. Squirrels feed on the ground and in the trees. They build nests on branches, and they play and hide in the treetops. You can see squirrels throughout the woods.

Cover: With its sharp claws, a young raccoon tries to hang on to a branch.

Published by The National Geographic Society, Washington, D.C.
Gilbert M. Grosvenor, *President*
Melvin M. Payne, *Chairman of the Board*
Owen R. Anderson, *Executive Vice President*
Robert L. Breeden, *Vice President, Publications and Educational Media*

Prepared by The Special Publications Division
Donald J. Crump, *Director*
Philip B. Silcott, *Associate Director*
William L. Allen, *Assistant Director*

Staff for this book
Jane H. Buxton, *Managing Editor*
John G. Agnone, *Picture Editor*
Jody Bolt, *Art Director*
Pamela J. Castaldi, *Designer*
Peggy D. Winston, *Researcher*
Carol Rocheleau Curtis, *Illustrations Assistant*
Elizabeth Ann Brazerol, Dianne T. Craven, Mary Elizabeth Davis, Eva Dillon, Rosamund Garner, Annie Hampford, Virginia W. Hannasch,
  Artemis S. Lampathakis, Cleo Petroff, Pamela Black Townsend, Virginia A. Williams, Eric Wilson, *Staff Assistants*

Engraving, Printing, and Product Manufacture
Robert W. Messer, *Manager*
George V. White, *Production Manager*
George J. Zeller, Jr., *Production Project Manager*
Mark R. Dunlevy, David V. Showers, Gregory Storer, *Assistant Production Managers;* Mary A. Bennett, *Production Assistant;*
  Julia F. Warner, *Production Staff Assistant*

Consultants
Lynda Bush, *Reading Consultant*
Cristol Fleming and Peter L. Munroe, *Educational Consultants*
Dr. Nicholas J. Long, *Consulting Psychologist*
Dr. Ronald M. Nowak, Office of Endangered Species, U.S. Fish and Wildlife Service, *Scientific Consultant*

Illustrations Credits
ANIMALS ANIMALS/Roger B. Minkoff (cover); ANIMALS ANIMALS/Oxford Scientific Films (1); Sisse Brimberg (2-3); ANIMALS ANIMALS/Lynn M.
Stone (3 lower); Leonard Lee Rue III (4-5, 6-7, 9, 10-11, 16-17, 26-27, 32); ANIMALS ANIMALS/Leonard Lee Rue III (5 right, 7 upper left, 8);
ANIMALS ANIMALS/E.R. Degginger (7 upper right); Jim Brandenburg (10, 14-15, 15 upper and lower, 18 upper and center); Annie Griffiths (12-13);
ANIMALS ANIMALS/Zig Leszczynski (18-19, 28-29); Jen and Des Bartlett (20, 22-23); ANIMALS ANIMALS/Charles Palek (21 left, 30 left, 30-31);
Tom and Pat Leeson (21 right, 24-25, 29 right); Steven C. Kaufman (25 lower left); National Geographic Photographer Bruce Dale (25 lower right).

Library of Congress CIP Data
  Eugene, Toni.
  Creatures of the woods.

  (Books for young explorers)
  Summary: Describes animals that may be found in forests and some of their activities.
  1. Forest fauna—Juvenile literature. [1. Forest animals] I. Title. II. Series.
QL112.E95 1985   591.909'.52   85-5129
ISBN 0-87044-560-X (regular edition)
ISBN 0-87044-560-0 (library edition)

MORE ABOUT Creatures of the Woods

The animals in *Creatures of the Woods* live in different kinds of forests and woods in North America. Woods are smaller than forests. Exploring either place can be an afternoon of discovery for you and your child. Trees offer shelter and food to a variety of creatures.

Any woodland is a community of many plants and animals that live together and interact. Much as a city contains people of all ages, types, sizes, and shapes, the woods are home to a multitude of creatures. Plants and animals live in various levels of a woods much as human tenants live on different floors of an apartment building.

The leafy crowns of the tallest trees form the canopy, the highest level of life in any woodland community. Crows and hawks roost and nest in this top floor of the woods. Warblers and other small birds forage from branch to branch.

Shorter, younger trees make up the understory, which is protected by the canopy. Squirrels (7, 32)* scamper throughout this level. Some songbirds build nests among the branches, and tree frogs search for insects there.

Shrubs and small trees form the next level of woodland life. Bears (18-21) and birds forage for berries in the shrub layer. In the herb layer, grasses, ferns, and wildflowers grow. Here, mice, insects, and snakes look for food, and female deer hide their newborn fawns.

On the floor of the woods, wild turkeys lay eggs in nests (4-5), and snakes (6-7) look for birds' eggs and

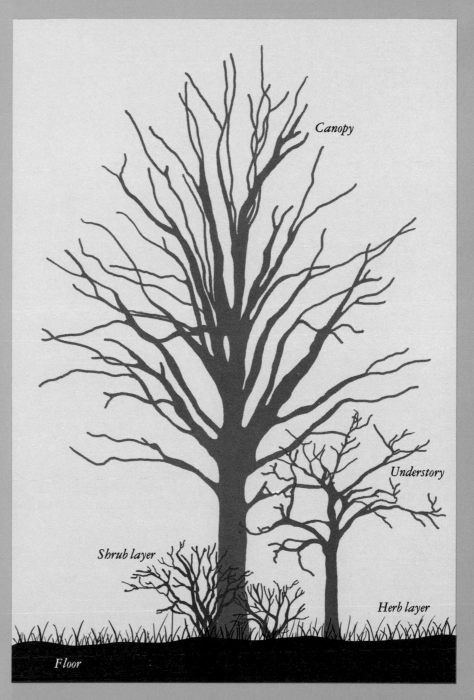

From the canopy to the floor, a forest holds several layers of life. Some birds nest in the tops of the tallest trees; others seek safety in the understory.
Deer nibble on the bark and branches of the shrub layer.
Rabbits eat grasses of the herb layer, and snakes slither on the forest floor.

*Numbers in parentheses refer to pages in *Creatures of the Woods*.

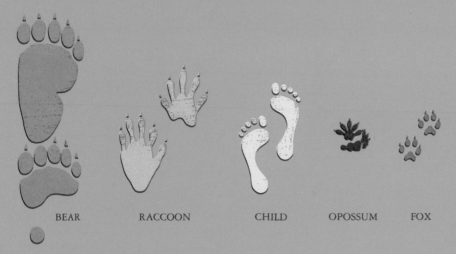

BEAR   RACCOON   CHILD   OPOSSUM   FOX

Telltale tracks can reveal which creatures hide in a woods.
You and your child may find some of these signs of life near streams
and ponds. Why do you think you would see them there?

small mammals. Slugs, millipedes, and earthworms crawl through the soil. Read about the woodland basement in *The World Beneath Your Feet,* another title in this set of Books for Young Explorers.

A complex web of life links all the plants and creatures of the woods. Caterpillars and other small insects, which eat tender plant leaves, are food for various birds. A grasshopper eating a leaf is itself a meal for a little tree frog, and that frog may be food for a raccoon (28-29). Squirrels and other rodents eat mainly plant material, such as leaves and nuts. They, in turn, are prey to such meat-eaters as owls (30-31), wolves (14-15), and raccoons (29).

There are always some creatures stirring in the woods. Most birds eat during the day and rest at night. Deer and rabbits feed in the hours around dawn and dusk. Opossums (26-27), raccoons, and owls hunt mainly at night.

Specially adapted eyes help owls and mountain lions (22-23) hunt in the dark. Creatures of the woods have adapted in other ways to life among the trees. Suction pads on the ends of their toes help tree frogs climb easily and cling to branches and leaves (28-29). The woodpecker has a strong bill that helps it pluck insects from

tree bark and chisel out holes in trees for its nest (9). An opossum's flexible paws and sharp claws help it climb.

You can share the wonders of the woods with your child. If there are trees near your house—in a park, off a country road, or even in a zoo—go there some afternoon and take a walk on the wild side. Remind your child that you may not see any animals at first. Explain that this is their home, and the animals know all the best hiding places.

But listen carefully, and you may hear the life of the woods. A breeze rustles the leaves above you. A woodpecker tap, tap, taps on a distant pine, and a cardinal sings its distinctive "purty, purty, purty."

Do you hear chattering? Glance up. An angry squirrel may be scolding you. Perhaps your child can find its nest of sticks and leaves high in the branches. Look carefully at the rest of the tree. Is there an owl's nest tucked in that hole in the trunk?

As you walk and listen, look around. Point out the ants and centipedes crawling on a dead log. Notice the delicate spider web stretched between two sticks. Near puddles or streams, or even in the snow, you may find the tracks of some woodland creatures. See if your child can

follow them. Perhaps they will lead to a chipmunk's home or even a fox's den. All around you there are signs of life. Deer may have nibbled the twigs, branches, or bark of trees. Do you see a hole in any of the trees? Could a woodpecker or a family of raccoons live there?

Rest together for a few minutes and wait very quietly. Can you hear the noises around you grow louder? If you sit still long enough, the animals will leave their hiding places and start back to work.

Birds will renew their search for food. A deer may wander past, or a rabbit may peek around a clump of grass. Residents of the woods will pass by all around you—scurrying across branches, crawling past your feet, crackling through the brush, and fluttering among the leaves.

For a few moments you may feel a part of the woodland community, as the creatures carry on their lives around you. If you move or make a sound, the spell will be broken. You are strangers in their world, and the animals quickly retreat. But you have introduced your child to the mood and magic of the woods. You can return some other day to learn more about the lives, habits, homes, and secret places of the creatures of the woods.

ADDITIONAL READING

America's Wild Woodlands. (Washington, D. C., National Geographic Society, 1985). Family reading.

How the Forest Grew, by W. Jaspersohn. (N.Y., Greenwillow Books, 1980). Ages 6-12.

See Through the Forest, by M. Selsam. (N.Y., Harper & Row, 1956). Ages 6-12.

Wildlife of the Forests, by A. and M. Sutton. (N.Y., Harry N. Abrams, Inc., 1979). Family reading.